Some of us take this world for granted, but there are ones who see the world as a blank canvas, ready to be transformed into a masterpiece. With the power of your perception, you can make anything possible. Sometimes life is unpredictable, but what you can control are your thoughts, emotions, and reactions. Your every action and thought are a stroke of your pencil, a small piece of a larger picture.

That's why we're here, to empower you to realize the true power of your mind and take control of your reality. Coloring is more than just a simple pastime, it's a kind of meditation, a way to connect with your inner creator.

Our mission is to guide you to a state of mind where the possibilities are limitless. In your hands, this tool can become a powerful technique for returning to the creator mode in life. Or it can simply be a source of joy and relaxation. The choice is yours, always yours.

So, let's color outside the lines, and let's make the world a more vibrant and beautiful place.

ArtZen Press

Thank you for choosing our Coloring book!

Welcome to ArtZen Press World, a publisher of beautiful coloring books
that will transport you to a world of creativity and relaxation.
Our mission is to empower you to be the creator of your reality
with our coloring books. By coloring with your own colors,
you tap into your innermost thoughts and emotions,
entering a state of creator.
The process becomes a meditative practice,
allowing you to explore the depths of your creativity.

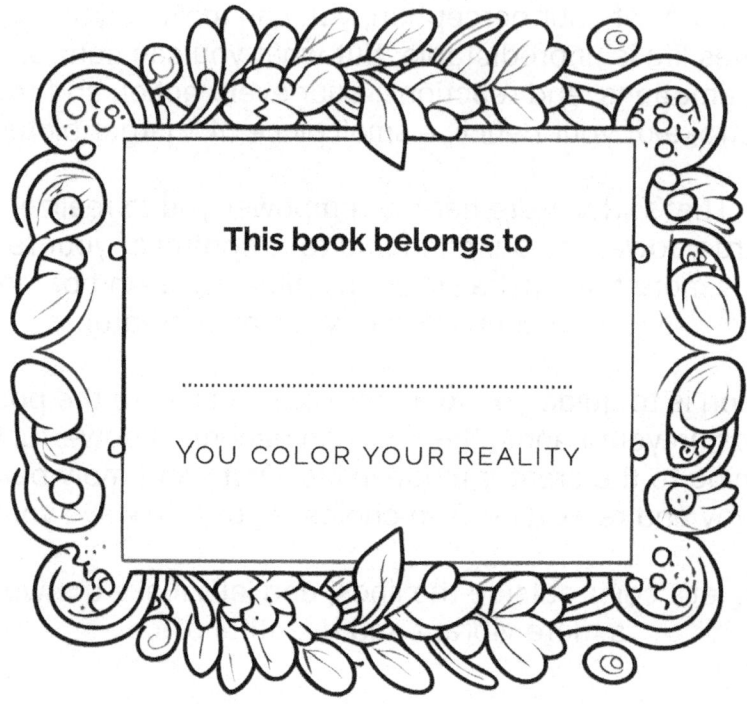

Copyright 2023 ArtZen Press all rights reserved.

Any reproduction or usage of this book without the author's written permission is strictly prohibited. However, private copyright is allowed. On the bright side, ArtZen Press grants you a whopping 200% permission to share your beautiful coloring art with the world!

When you use this book Amazon offers paper
selections that are best suited for colored pencils
and alcohol-based markers.

To prevent any bleed-through, it is recommended to use
a sheet of paper behind the page when using wet mediums.

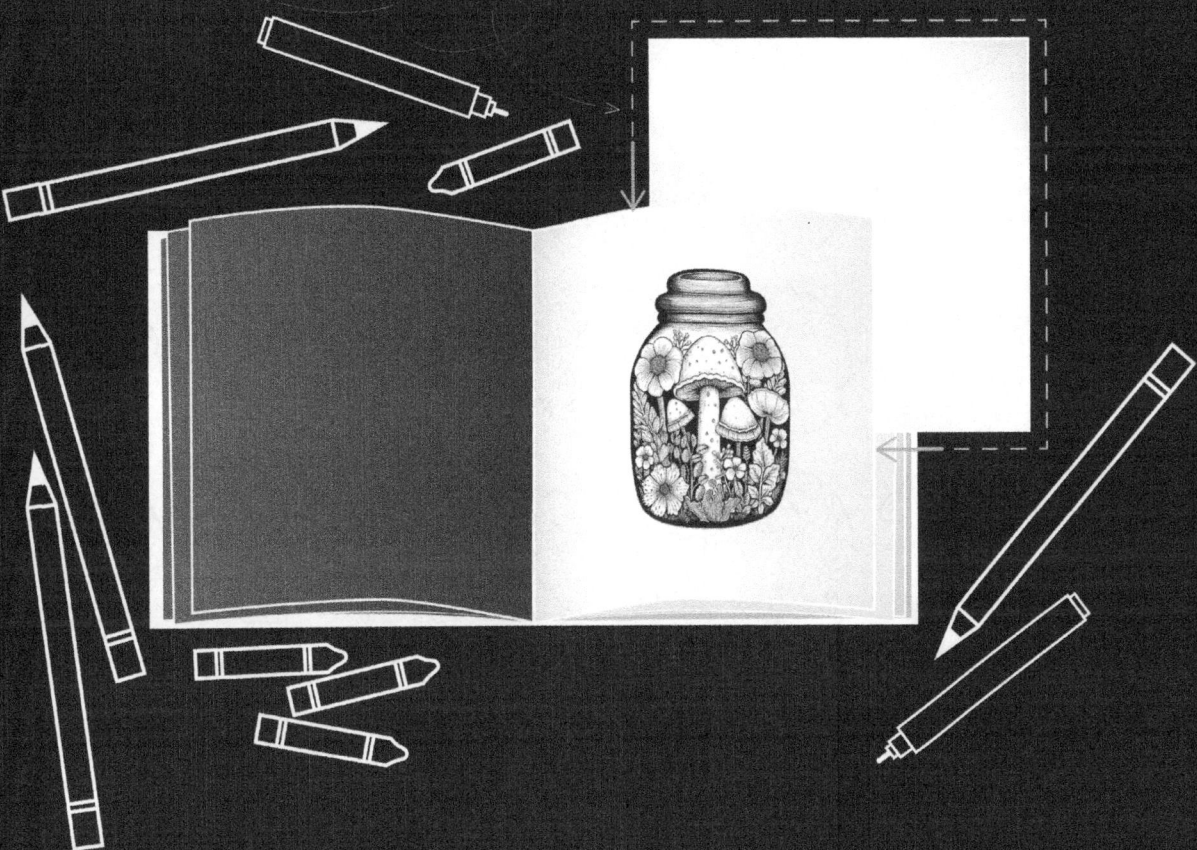

When you finish coloring
Please share your honest opinion on Amazon
It will enable us to become better
Have a question? Let us know
Artzen.books@gmail.com

TEST YOUR COLORS

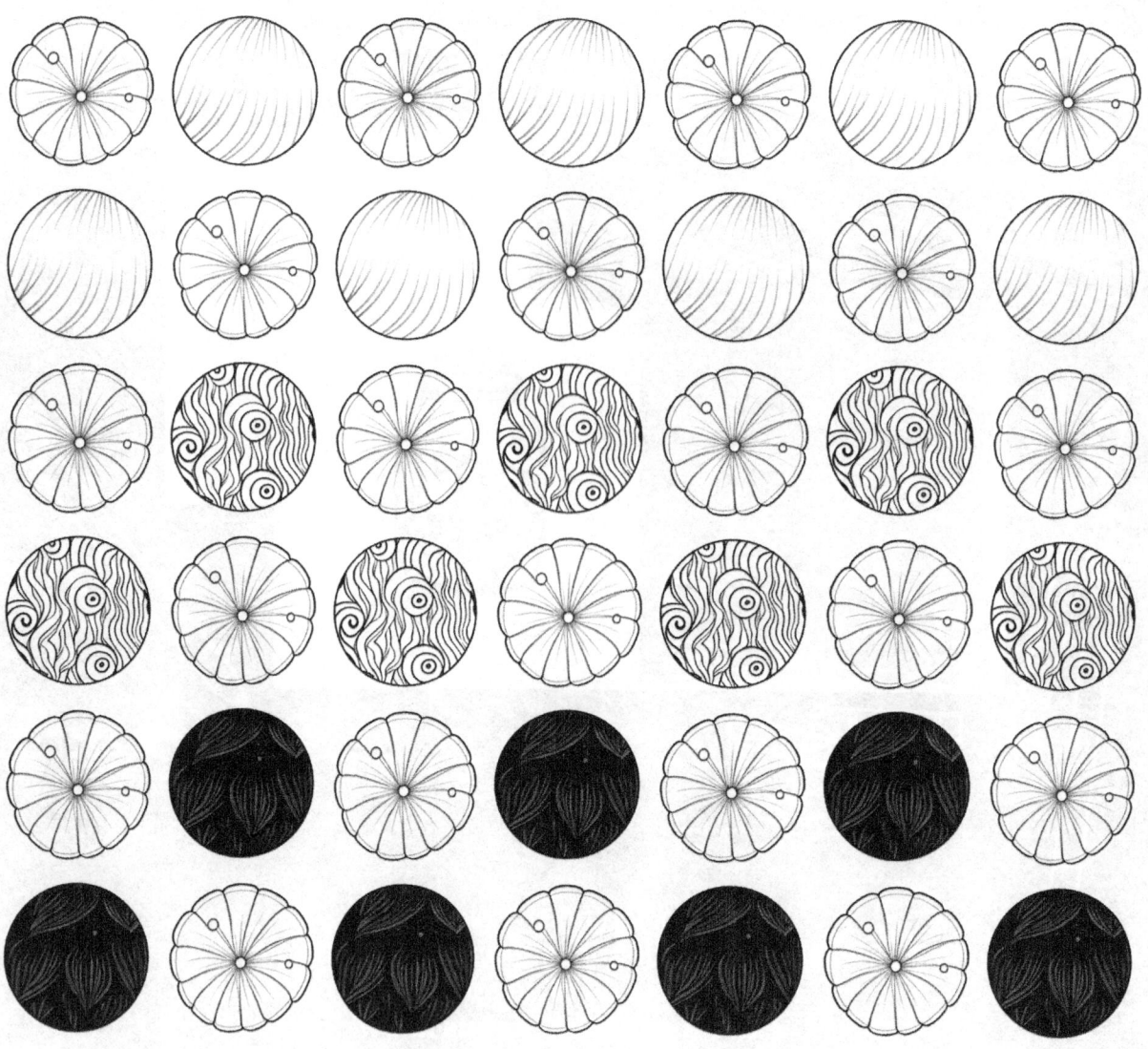

Believe in yourself and your unique vision.

Inspiration
is all around us,
we just have
to open our eyes
and look.

Imagination is the key to unlocking creativity.

*Create
from the heart
and let your
imagination
soar.*

Focus on
what you
can control,
and let go
of what you can't.

The greatest inspiration comes from within, so trust your instincts and follow your passions.

Keep practicing and experimenting to hone your craft.

Inspiration is the spark that ignites creativity and innovation.

Your imagination is your greatest asset.

Embrace your uniqueness and let it shine through your art.

A clear mind leads to clear results.

Surround yourself with people who inspire and support you.

Don't be afraid
to take risks
and try
new things.

Imagination allows us to see the world in a different light.

Concentration is the key to unlocking your full potential.

Stay inspired by seeking out new experiences and perspectives.

Without imagination, we would be limited to the world as it is.

Seek out
new experiences
and challenges
to fuel
your inspiration.

Believe in yourself and your ability to create something amazing.

Small distractions can lead to big setbacks, so stay focused.

Inspiration is not just a feeling, it's a mindset that can be cultivated and nurtured.

Inspiration
can come
from anywhere,
keep your eyes
and mind open.

The ability to concentrate is a skill that can be developed and honed.

Set goals and work towards them with purpose and determination.

Stay curious
and never stop learning,
inspiration
will follow.

Set achievable goals and concentrate on one task at a time.

Trust the creative process and allow yourself to make mistakes.

The limits of your imagination are the only limits to your possibilities.

Find ways
to tap into your creativity,
whether
it's through art,
music, writing,
or other forms
of expression.

Perfection is not the goal, progress is.

Inspiration can come from failure, use setbacks as fuel for your next big idea.

Remember that creativity is a journey, not a destination.

Imagination is the foundation of all great ideas.

Surround yourself with positivity and optimism, inspiration thrives in a positive environment.

Concentration is not just about working harder, but working smarter.

Inspiration is contagious, share your ideas and collaborate with others.

Keep creating, even when it's difficult or challenging.

Imagination is the source of innovation and progress.

Your art
has the power
to change
the world,
so keep creating.

Embrace
the unknown
and take risks,
nspiration often comes
from
stepping outside
your comfort zone.

Take breaks when needed to recharge your mind and increase concentration.

The future belongs to those who can imagine it.

Creativity is a muscle, the more you use it, the stronger it becomes.

Train your mind to stay focused, and you'll achieve more than you ever thought possible.

Inspiration is a journey, not a destination, enjoy the process and keep moving forward.

Believe in yourself and your ability to create something amazing, inspiration is just the beginning.

Inspiration
is a reminder
that anything is possible,
so dream big
and never give up
on your vision.

Relaxation is not a luxury, it's a necessity for a healthy mind and body.

Made in the USA
Monee, IL
18 September 2023